# B IS FOR BEAR: BEARS FACTS FOR KIDS

Like human children,
bear cubs are
extremely playful.

Bears are found on the continents of North America, South America, Europe, and Asia.

Bears
are large
mammals that
eat mostly
meat and
fish, with the
exception of
panda bears
which are
herbivores
and live also
entirely on
bamboo.

Bear cubs are born in litters of 1 to 3 and usually stay with their mothers for about 3 years.

Bears have excellent senses of smell, sight and hearing. They can run very fast and are also good at climbing and swimming.

Bears have
a large brain
and are one
of the more
intelligent
mammals.

Bears care deeply about family members. They will risk their lives and even fight to the death in order to save a cub or sibling from danger.

Bears take
a long sleep
in the winter
similar to
hibernation.
They will sleep
in their dens
and a mother
bear will also
have her cubs
in a den.